COUNTRY, LIVING

a collection of poems

COUNTRY, LIVING

a collection of poems

IRA SADOFF

Alice James Books
Farmington, Maine
www.alicejamesbooks.org

© 2020 by Ira Sadoff
All rights reserved
Printed in the United States

10 9 8 7 6 5 4 3 2 1

Alice James Books are published by Alice James Poetry Cooperative, Inc.,
an affiliate of the University of Maine at Farmington.

Alice James Books
114 Prescott Street
Farmington, ME 04938
www.alicejamesbooks.org

Library of Congress Cataloging-in-Publication Control Number: 2019050945

Alice James Books gratefully acknowledges support from individual donors, private foundations, the University of
Maine at Farmington, the National Endowment for the Arts, and the Amazon Literary Partnership.

Cover art: Image from Bleak House Series © 2011 Graeme Webb

Contents

2.

3.

ACKNOWLEDGMENTS

Earlier versions of the following poems appeared in:

Academy of American Poets' Poem-a-Day series: "A Few Surprising Turns"
(reprinted in *Columbia Daily Tribune*), "Ithaca," "Old Selves"

Agni: "Broken Sonnet for the Universe," "Indiana"

American Poetry Review: "1988" (now "Lost"), "In My Dream," "My
Tulsa," "Nothing" (now "This Once"), "Ode to the Defense Mechanism,"
"Old World/New World," "Thelonious Monk of Weehawken"

Blackbird: "Self-Portrait with Michelangelo," "Interior with Mickey
Mantle"

Chattahoochee Review: "The Word Beautiful"

Colorado Review: "The Future"

The Enchanting Verses Literary Review: "In the Aviary"

The New Yorker: "I Never Needed Things"

Plume: "By the Meadows of Hay Bales" "In the House of Wittgenstein,"
"Self-Portrait with Bill Evans at the Vanguard," "Shhhh!"

(now "Self-Portrait with Hawthorne in the Rearview Mirror"),
"Wilderness"

The Plume Anthology of Poetry 5: "I Apologize in Advance," "Deathbed
Confession"

Prairie Schooner: "The Veneer" (now "Los Angeles, Downtown: 1958")

Salamander: "Emendation," "Stranded on Old US 1, Wrens, Georgia"

Tin House: "Biographical Sketch," "The Defeat of Brooklyn"

*This book is dedicated to Liza Henderson, who means more
to me than words can say, and dear friends Gerald Stern
and Adrian Blevins, who read the manuscript, offered valuable
criticism and invaluable encouragement and praise.*

1.

MY DESIGN

For every complex problem
there is a solution that is clear, simple, and wrong.

—H.L. Mencken

BIOGRAPHICAL SKETCH

I've been a soft touch, a rough ride, I took shots
at congressmen, left an outrageous tip
for a waif whose hand was shaking

as she poured my tea. I made the sound of a wolf
in Naomi's bedroom, was shabby
at her wedding, sulking

while pinning an amorous note
to her gown. I refused to cross a picket line
then bought a handsome silk shirt

sewn in the most downtrodden district in China.
This when I was learning how to be a person,
which even now's an unfinished symphony.

But no one warned me about the solemn passages,
when we know no one, when we could die
far from home with our bungled furies and crushes

yammering beside us: *Not yet, not yet.*

I NEVER NEEDED THINGS

I never loved a shiny car, longed for
the Azores, cashmere sweaters
to make life matter more. I don't need

that great cabernet, though *Chateau Montelena*
sends me back to a pond, a vineyard picnic—
the woman I'm with, she's a different story.

I always saw my family life as a sinkhole
I tried to climb out of. But more
it was a vacuum, a grave that needed dirt

to fill it in. So stuck was I, I wanted only
to tag along, to hold onto someone for the ride.
I'm still not sure how to conduct myself.

Does anyone? So many selves craving
to be seen and cared for. Once in a while
I drive to a mall to peer in shop windows,

to see what the excitement's about.
A mother tries a dress on her daughter,
a young man chooses between TV screens.

They seem at home here. Sometimes
I think their joy is sensual: they find little gems
in the earth shining. I want to take home

their expressions, wear them awhile.

A FEW SURPRISING TURNS

Ultimately the air
Is bare sunlight where must be found
The lyric valuables

—George Oppen

A few surprising turns follow us everywhere.
I was shopping for something to replace
what I once felt. Weren't there buildings where
we once lived, fully furnished, that looked out
over the river? A festival somewhere? At the core
we were traipse and meander, lacking a clock
when we ran into a war
and some items to love. A lovely vintage teapot
and a stash of old photographs
where unhappiness could be scored. But that's
not the tale we share. It takes more than two tongues
to bring us forward, to where we could shine
just by recalling a few useless details—
as if in school—the capitol of Nebraska,
the acid formula for vinegar,
the day my father walked out the door.

ODE TO THE DEFENSE MECHANISM

Some of the deadpan comes from the flatness,
the feigned all-rightness, the sickening thrum of Kansas,
taking all day to drive through that treelessness.

Inside the hardness of the heart, the numbness
of the heart, there lay a smaller heart,
a splinter in your finger, throbbing and pulsing

so you can see how alive you are. God
what a fenestration the heart is.
What strangers find is frontismatter,

an intro to the highlights as we see them.
All our old loves are still there,
impervious and glass-enclosed. You can tap

on the glass and get a rise out of them
because into each life there must be
a ruler and a grid, a little *schadenfreude*

so it won't be our hearts breaking.

5

INDIANA

All the tales I tell of Indiana are cheerful
and glazed with morals, by which I mean

I fell in love on a porch swing in Indiana.
Weekends were sprinkled with fireflies

and crickets. If I coughed, neighbors
boiled me jars of jam. Home of the plow

and pigsty, the KKK, wigs in church.
Nevertheless, everything good in me

comes from Indiana, except nights
I escaped to Kentucky, to bars

where God appeared as a worm
in a tequila glass. I sang to him

of my shame, secular and defended.
I mean no one in Indiana understood me,

except a hermit thrush and a wood thrush.
With their panpipes, double voice boxes,

how lyrical they were, how righteous,
singing sweetly to both sides of the story.

BY THE MEADOWS OF HAY BALES

By the meadows of hay bales
and daffodils, of corn husks and pig shit,
in a forgettable little hamlet

in sincere Indiana, my retreat
from the world, I forgot how gloomy
I was, choosing for company

insects and voles. There I was
spared the satisfactions
of great ambitions. A good plan

to live by: I survived a tornado,
a marriage, a war, a leveled panorama
after every harvest. A little heaven

with no one near. Many loved
the sheen of cheerfulness,
but the animal in me kept on growling.

SELF-PORTRAIT AS A FOREIGN BODY

There's Grief of Want— and grief of Cold —
A sort they call "Despair" —
There's Banishment from native Eyes —
In sight of Native Air

        —Emily Dickinson

The Lord is my shield and horn
of my salvation, and I'm sick of it. Maybe Dexter Gordon
didn't mind playing the same riffs from 1949
to his dying day, but I wanted to live in a different body,
wanted to be wed to someone else. I was steady,
you could count on me: that was my excuse.
When they took his cabaret card away he flew
to Denmark, where he couldn't hear Trane or Ornette
so he played the same old riffs: "Body and Soul,"
"Sweet Lorraine," tunes I couldn't get out of my head
in a country that was nothing but flatlands
and a few tiny islands bobbing up and down.

HEAVEN AND HELL

I've never been afraid of heaven or hell.
I've had my own versions, like you.

My gods were frenzy, ruckus, and delirium.
My sin: loving the tongue too much.

I had my devotions, my book of hymns:
I could praise the curve of her shoulder,

hail her genius, pour so much into her.
In one of those states, who cares

about an afterlife? This life overflows
the way a thaw floods a muddy river.

The banks were swampy. I was
untethered, a trifle in the scheme of things.

I can't plead a special case. But if
you hovered over this earth you'd hear

hearts like mine hammer in that disarray.
We are not faithless, we who unfasten

so easily. We, the Friends of Aftermath.

LOST

for Chet Baker

The whole story seemed slipshod,
from working the docks of Ancona
to chasing Chet all over the country—
he was desolate, emaciated, playing
all smears and blurs, shooting up once

in the cathedral of San Ciriaco.
He was my teacher, but it wasn't music
I was after, it was a mood—
black ink, where they held him over
the edge of a balcony, shaking

the change out of him, finally dropping him
a story or two. And where was I then,
the biography of no interest
beyond raising up massive wooden boxes
of cargo, coffins shipped from one no place

to another? Our connection: *How do I get
what's coming to me?* The Roman arches,
the view of the sea so blue you
could almost forgive the leaden afternoons
after work, with no one to do in the bars:

I had no art to speak of. He at least
was beautiful once, boyish, sweet-voiced:
everybody wanted him. His story was stupid,
a romance of squalor, but I wanted to steal it.
I had before me that one perfect night

in Recanati, his last, ideal as I remember it.
His "I Thought about You" completely parenthetical,
on pitch, full of ideas he got from Miles,
but it shook me enough to send me back to the States.
When the set was over he smiled, toothless, at all six of us.

I mean we didn't want to die then, being human.

SELF-PORTRAIT WITH HAWTHORNE
IN THE REARVIEW MIRROR

We walked in the woods, like Dimmesdale and Hester,
but back then I didn't give a shit about literature:
there was this woman who adored me:
probably she didn't know me, she confused me
with some antidote to her self-absorbed boyfriend.
Maybe she saw the two of us as the same person.
Later she'd join some sexless sect that wore
white robes and burned incense—she was mixed-up
with a deceitful husband and tons of debt,
and I had my own heartbreak, better not to mention.
I remember her round face and her curly hair
and some exact phrases: we told secrets, we groused:
Who cared about us? So let me open up
the world a little because this is getting claustrophobic:
we'd invaded tiny countries, the Clintons
had locked up the poor, and in spite of her humiliations—
Bill's affairs, her brightness casting shadows
on every bloviating congressman—she praised the Defense
of Marriage Act. That's all I knew and I could get agitated about it,

but don't forget we were sitting on a log by a stream,
no one saw us, we could have kept on going
to a deeper and darker place—but how much more time
did we have to waste before we'd become irretrievably bereft,
basking in decay, when the woods just needed scrubbing.
Maybe if we'd gotten on our knees
and made a square of meadow, lilies of the valley—
with their upside-down little white bells—
might shoot up out of nowhere.

WHY DO WE MAKE UP THINGS?

Why do we make up things when there's so much to savor
on our block, where the five-star jasmine scent
is tropical and inescapable, and the gardeners, Hispanic

and Ethiopian, are on their knees for us, pulling
and tugging at the earth, speaking several languages at once,
so far from home they double-time their dreaming?

A reverie might transport them to their favorite almendro.
In that shade they might dream of their wives
when they have no wives, or double back to a dreaded barbershop,

because now they want their hair touched, and their cheeks.
They want the salt rubbed out with a handkerchief.
How would I describe the air they breathe? There's so much else,

from the Kuku Sebsebe love song they can't stop humming
to the gardening they do because I'm never home,
so can't name a dozen plants that bloom in my own backyard.

Why do I colonize their thoughts and labor?

16

Must every gesture be accounted for? Must it be "held up
to the light," and by held up I mean stopped at the border,
frisked, photographed, detailed, approaching
the suspect as you might a stranger?
Maybe we make up things to figure out the great

divide, when to cross it. But more to be on fire,
to acquire the chops of McCoy Tyner,
the loving skills of Ghandi, to go on and on like that.

SELF-PORTRAIT WITH MICHELANGELO

In the Star Theater of Rome, NY, I paint ceilings
on the ladder to heaven where the air is thin.
After a few brush strokes I sit on the top rung
to savor the figures of light and shadow on screen.

I'll want to save them—but also send some to islands
where they can't beguile or terrify. It's a revelation
to come out of the theater so absorbed by their voices
and grimaces, these acts of creation, translucent as we are,

substantial and eternal, a state of mind the body
can't kill off, as when Liza's away on Guadeloupe,
muse to herself only, I conjure her sketching a waterfall,
eating cassava and christophine, hoarding perfumes

and scarves in Port-à -Pitre. She's all flashes
and cloudbursts, there's infinitesimal movement
between the frames so you can't register
the changes. I call her Liza so you're attached to her

and the name Liza: she has reddish brown hair
and green eyes, smiles too much and loves to swim
too close to sharks. I don't want her
swallowed up by life itself. Because she's

a complete stranger I'm endlessly curious:
isn't that love, knowing and not knowing,
framing a gesture to make her familiar?
I make everything up: her jasmine scent,

the delicate powder on the screen of her forehead,
but how can I paint the streets and their screens,
to come back to earth with the darkness it deserves,
where I live with my ordinary friends, the divine?

WILDERNESS

Just yesterday, when I came upon
a snow-patched meadow
above the tree line—the air so thin
my hike left me out of breath—
in this green, unkempt site
just off the map, I saw a pond with moose,
cows and bulls in a fangle
slurping at its edge until some sound stirred them.

How clumsy and rushed their exit,
and what a cluttered music their hooves made
on the granite ledge. That set off
the magpies warbling and screeching
like a sea of cicadas. I couldn't tell you
where I was, I can't describe
the jumble of sensations, the dizzying changes
in the light, clouds appearing, passing,
shading my whole field of vision. It all
just slid into my horizon without raising a finger.

I come from the land of laments and heavy lifting.

The apostle Paul and I, we both worked hard to please a god,

if not a god then someone divine, and I could say we were both blinded,

but really there's just very little light and shadow at dusk,

so I went back to the husk of my car, the meaning

still sealed in my body: I couldn't climb out of it

to raise up the unspeakable: I couldn't

bring it to my throat so I kept it with me.

MEDITATION

I could use a better roll with the punches disposition.
I should sit on my prayer rug and welcome the stillness
but I'm in a frenzy with all that flashes before me,
whether it's a field of asters or a ring in a drawer
with a face attached to it that sends me
to the separate bedrooms, the silence
not even the dead know. But soon you'll be
dead to me, soon I'll block out the good days,
the canals of Venice, the carafes and their refills,
the swirling dusty trails that led to the bottom of the canyon.
And how did we find waterfalls, and how did we forget
to have children, and why did we waste all those afternoons
on a tiny couch—it was a loveseat after all—
explaining ourselves to someone who'd heard it all before,
the bruises of love, then come out into the moonlight of February.

2.

MY COUNTRY

BROKEN SONNET FOR THE UNIVERSE

I know I'm worth fifteen cents to the universe.
I don't know a thing about you-name-it.
But if the world were still made of brightness
and shades of green, surfaces that flutter
and turn to stillness, perhaps we would not live
like starlings, devouring everything
from seeds to insects, from fruits to carrion.
Maybe we need more planets to use up
and toss aside. Forget the green palm leaves
of the Amazon, but if we lose the marsh,
the rails and bitterns, if we lose the stream bed
and thirsty trees that lean over the water,
how dry this universe, how ghostly, how gone.

OLD WORLD/NEW WORLD

My friends, the parameters were missing.

I was on a bad tributary.
How thorny were those branches?
Down the road the desultory frontier of ocean
was scathing. No, that was someone

I'd cared for. Cared for, monitored, patrolled.
How many sides to a story?
Left with a scythe to cut through the brush
to pass from one world, not merely

from the first scream into the wilderness,
but what we've shot through and unfastened.
The country is not a person. Nevertheless
I must be close to dead center, no longer sure

who speaks for me, why my voice breaks:

gunfire everywhere, and by gunfire
I mean gunfire, words as weapons, take-overs,
conquests, fevers…weren't we
original once, before grief, before sequence,

somewhere between the first and last breath?

MY TULSA

in Tornado Alley, where the ground opens up
once in a while before it seals back up,
you get a few glimpses, an upskirt of the city.
What was once home of lovers' quarrels
became black neighborhoods, aerial bombings.

What was once home of the Lochapoka
is now the hokey-pokey. Not much I make of this,
this before my time, this *I didn't do it*.
Except everything is glued to me, nailed there
on a poster. In Tulsa I am alone. True,

in a *who cares* kind of way. More feeling
I'd been planted in someone else's country.
I mean the way I strode, tilted my head, little jokes
I told cashiers never even brought a stare.
So I thought of cities where we fix our attention

on the sidewalk, not to be penetrated by leers,
not to let strangers see how years
have twisted our expressions. Oil told the story here,
the way the Triangle fire told the story
of the Weinbergs, Greenspans, and Cohens. I stood

on that corner at Washington Place last year:
there too when I closed my eyes, ashes stirred the air.

THE DEFEAT OF BROOKLYN

I'm white inside, but that don't help my case
'cause I can't hide what is on my face
　　　　　—Louis Armstrong, "Black and Blue"

George Washington and I were dining at the Inn after the Defeat of Brooklyn.
He was a mopey little icon, the object of some scrutiny.
Since his lips were pursed I couldn't tell if his teeth were made of wood.
I tried to cheer him up with talk of America's future: couldn't he hear
the ka-ching ringing from the skies? Soon we'd be all hope
and avarice, our troops overseas, our little hamburgers everywhere.

When Washington decreed no Black could fight in his Army,
he had no idea I was black. I mean inside out, which is what we white
　　people think,
for we too had been beaten, have been slaves to buying and selling,
　　we too hated our masters, whether they were bankers
or Trustees of the Court. That's the case I was making, because *liar,*
appropriator, solipsist, out of our hands, these were the lessons

we took from homeschooling. A thousand men left for dead. The army
split in two, and—just so you know—next time you sit
in Battery Park staring at women's asses, you might want to thank Washington
for knocking off some of your ancestors (before you go back to the office).
Lunch hour was almost over, and we were both in a black mood,

which made the drinking easy. When I got up to pee

I thought to myself this guy's so famous no one will remember me
unless I snap the two of us together. We of the same country.

LOS ANGELES, DOWNTOWN: 1958

When I think of veneer, a surface or facade,
I think of the peeling panel on her bathroom door,
how you could look in as she doused herself with a sponge.
The old train station in Los Angeles, police sweeps

through the skeletal remains of five and tens
(how far apart we are, public and private sectors)
and closer to home, I watched her forge her lipstick,
shaking before she goes out, rehearsing in the mirror,

assembling the costume she's seen in a department store—
and you know what we think of mannequins—
downing valium and Manhattans, the actress carting around
her character, where some fragment, some broken sliver

of her is lodged in a lipstick smudge, a little blood
trickling out. And I might even shift in my seat,
knowing how my face absorbs and refracts
that light, and as the camera pans in on the closer-yet,

the distance between the surface of that adolescent face
and what *it feels like* to me seems abysmal,
as her doctor said, *Psychosis is personal*;
how her hand shaking becomes way too personal

as she puts on a string of pearls of water, flour, and paste
I made for her, because we've taken a wrong turn
somewhere (because the "good providers"
of the fifties have driven to the end of the century)

and now I remember the story of her mother,
ferreting through the debris of her bombed-out
Warsaw apartment, searching for her husband, hauling
on her back a hardback chair, a vanity of oak veneer.

BECAUSE BY THIS TIME

for Rosie Green

she had so much disease in her, was so fevered,
we could no longer think of her as a cipher,
a cup we could drink from. I say we

because we all come from the same anteroom,
the same hospital bed. When I was born
she sang to me through the glass. At the Lighthouse

I heard her sing once or twice: she had chops galore
and younger singers went to school on her.
You don't know her, but if you know west coast jazz

then you know the chill to it, repressed and sunny.
She opened up to no one. If no one gave her
a chance to record, if no one cared how she'd survive,

then no one wants to hear about wild gestures
conducted from the rails of her bed. But
the tenderness I'd always longed to feel for her

surfaced when I saw her face. I saw everything
in her lips moving without a sound,
and was suddenly glad to be born, breathing,

included in a scene where we sanctioned feeling,
even glorified it—so we who'd turned
from her could take one more thing: her voice.

IN THE CURRENT CLIMATE

An unrelenting snow, a dazzling snow,
the streets whitened and chilled, bleak and pure,
a thin white scarf on tree limbs, psalms
of white flakes descending. How mesmerizing:
you can't tell the road from the meadow.
I suppose the chilled hopes of Mandelstam
might have bloomed if he'd kept them
from his government, if he'd kept in his head
his manifestos where no one could find them.
Did you ever shout in a snow storm, scared
they'd come for you? Not likely. But
elsewhere many are sent away:
you can hear the tearing whispers
holding back their cries so they can stay
in what once we called a sanctuary.

STRANDED ON OLD US 1, WRENS, GEORGIA

Steam rose from the old black Ford.
You could see where the engine block had cracked,
but not where the auto industry hit the wall—
good-bye DeSoto, good-bye Edsel,
good-bye factory jobs, payrolls, and little shops.
Good-bye father's office. You could see him
by the radiator boiling over, but who saw
the Midwest dying, who saw China?
They stood there thinking *Why me?*
staring into the swirl of the unfixable,
into the vortex of breakdowns to come.
Whose job was it to paint surfaces
with joy, to repair the universe
for our ne'er-do-wells, our helpless neighbors,
hardworking dreamers who dreamed their dreams
in the wrong year, in the wrong country?

ONCE WAS

Gone are the days of my mistress,
my mother, my little girl, my concubine,
my country, my empire, so that's
something to be grateful for. But I miss
the manufacturing jobs of the fifties
and the big elm trees fraught with disease,
department store windows with Nativity Scenes,
and loved that sinful feeling
when you ordered a frappe with your burger.
We who survived those suburbs
and saw so few caveats,
we are lost little souls—with sorrow,
that's how we'd paint our faces.

THIS ONCE

A sheltered cove sent me the gift of stillness.
It almost seemed a crime to breathe.
Then my cottage had to be filled with joy.
A Haydn symphony. I trimmed the fresh asparagus,
poured a wine, all floral and mineral.
And the tulips I planted last fall, their bouquet
was bounty for my Chinese vase.
I needed a city or some mountain town
where I'd arrive by donkey. It would be Italy,
with olive groves and the kind of summer heat
that pressed your cheeks like a mother's palm.
Not the mother I was given, not the father
whose excitement was extreme, delusional.
I can love them now that they're missing
but I won't forget how our restless souls
took the tour bus from our holiday.

ODE TO FORGETFULNESS

I never saw how gone he was
though was told he drifted like a skiff

along the narrow streets of Venice,
dismayed by the should-have-beens

and could-have-beens
he remembered for a minute,

but mostly there was a traffic jam
of thoughts, that's what I'm told occurs

when the mind burns off
its old possessions. On the last day

of the Aztec ceremony they
set fire to every stick of furniture

to assure the world would last
another fifty years. Good-bye, father,

you who left so long ago: can I
mourn how gone you've been?

INTERIOR WITH MICKEY MANTLE

The bones, they were brittle
and breaking. Drink, my friend, brought me back
to dusty Oklahoma, home of my dead father,
and someone I once called myself. I was drawing a blank.
Nothing left in storage, nothing but a banked expression
I painted on. I needed a liaison, someone to trigger
a little cheer, some exultation. I never knew,
what were wives for? What were people for?
What was I for? Does it matter how boring
baseball is, how boring I am, how we keep making
the same mistakes, dressing them differently?
Aren't there moments we realize
what little shits we are, minding our own business,
making the world a worse place by example,
preening and whining? When you've lived your life
as someone else's dream of you? Statues,
that's what we become,
with a few Easter lilies left behind
by those who celebrate their favorite stranger.

IN MY DREAM

I worried about my daughter,
so I was shaken awake
because I have no daughter, and whatever
knowing looks, whatever cakes
we could have baked together, whatever gifts
we could grant one another, they were
slipping out of sight, the way parents do,
to those who belong only to the world
of writing and thinking. There was no body there.
Of course there'd have been bribes,
chastisements, attention-getting manipulations:
but whose would they be? There was a trampoline,
maybe a carousel, a clumsy gesture....
I was raising her up so she could see:
it was a nightmare. A nightmare I tell you, a nightmare.

OLD SELVES

Ok, I no longer want them,
the many selves I had to manage

that exhausted everyone. I believed in
angels then, thought I might be

one—that would be me,
flying off on a tangent, just to land

on someone's balcony.
But so little could I see from there

I longed for company
with wings: too often I took flight

just to feel the air slap my cheek.

IN THE PUBLIC SPHERE

First there's the inflation factor, the making too much of,
the syllogism, some absent third partner
making decisions on the big board,
wherefore meanwhile in spite of but and because
all taking their toll. You might look
into the epicenter, where cars have fallen in
after the mudslide, where we sleep in our separate cinemas.
Our chatter too is meandering, vague, stolen
from a secondary source. There must be some site
on earth where we still matter to the animals
and the outline of hills, where buying and selling
have pulled up stakes. I'm famished for a simple sentence
that proceeds from subject to verb to object
without turning into the driveway
of a celebrity, looking up her dress. Otherwise
there's just the afterlife, that dizzy hit-your-head-on-the-ceiling
feeling, bright lights followed by hymns
that beseech you to get on your knees and surrender.

ODE TO INCOME INEQUALITY

In my favorite Maserati I made a difference.
For those of you reading this in another century,
it's incomprehensible, isn't? I mean all of it,
from the dollar counting more
than Luther could sin for, to talking on your mobile
while checking your favorite recipe, fretting days away
because we can't compete with the ocean
or the bay's dazzling the last moments of sunlight.
And why not say resplendent if that's what you mean?
And why not say my father was my hero
until I saw how insatiable we were for all things shiny.
Once I packed my bags to head for Norway,
where if things go wrong no one hears about it,
because mistakes had been made, bad ones too,
from bomb-dropping to that unfathomable wedding day,
all because we're so mucked up with quagmires,
unforeseen impasses and entanglements.
So just to be safe we shut our doors. Alternatively
I'd like to prove the human being is more than a segue
between centuries: yes we have hearts, even if we store them
in vaults like hostages in bad movies, very bad movies.

PATRIOT

I need a new lens
to view the sordid whatnots
of my government. Dense and dreary
with flashes of fireworks and manly displays
of encroachment and invasion,
that's what got us here.
What a body of work we've become,
taking over bars, defending our favorite countries,
inspiring dread and dismay
and enough agitation so when I board a plane
to fly over the mayhem we've made
I come back to the blunder debacle compartment
prepared to endorse everything faulty,
meager, wanting. Then I remember
the founder of this country and the slaves
he owned. In his very lengthy will
he freed the one who brought him his housecoat
and tea. That's the Washington
I want to remember.

III.

In many shamanic societies, if you came to a medicine person complaining
of being disheartened, dispirited, or depressed, they would ask you one of
four questions: When did you stop dancing? When did you stop singing?
When did you stop being enchanted by stories? When did you stop
finding comfort in the sweet territory of silence?

—GABRIELLE ROTH, *Maps to Ecstasy*

IN THE HOUSE OF WITTGENSTEIN

The limits of my language mean the limits of my world.
—Ludwig Wittgenstein

He never saw the malls of Petaluma, nor met the amazing cricketer Montezuma. He never heard a laugh track. We'd like to see him stroke a cat wrapped in a kaftan. Let him find a mechanic for our mufflers. Or raise sandbags in Port-au-Prince.

Only once did he eat a plantain and in his notebook describe the process as sloshing through the Everglades.

Otherwise he was a word hotel. His best friend was a hut in Norway.

Maybe he was smart enough for a table of twelve. He could play all twelve parts.

What's to be done with a man who lives in his head? Ira, my friend, are you listening?

THELONIOUS MONK OF WEEHAWKEN

There are no wrong notes.
                    —Thelonious Monk

In the third set
of Monk's last gig, the same tunes
he'd played since 1950
rocked a little something inside us.

Had we been there
when his fingers first stirred things up,
we might have bowed
to his off-key thumping. But since

we came late, we heard
the notes one by one as they appeared
in all their likenesses,
in all their lessness: of course we thought

there'd be a next. But he
was a madman really, denuded, helpless,
dazed. What I'm saying,
dear gods, is don't send our old loves back:

that first Picasso, the beauty
who treated us to months of sugary pleasure—
I don't want to know
what she's become. When we look at our own

faces I wish we could love
them more. It's too easy to forget the scored,
the weathered, old
houses with character, the ancient cliffs

of the Palisades where our Monk last lived.

TROPICAL

Whatever was florid, ornamental,
soporific, whatever turned only to the light,
whatever was a swimsuit and a splash of Tequila,
whatever was all chimera, Maya, a magic trick,
I was there to bless it, to long for it.
I was there under the palm, I was there alone
and I was there with a margarita,
I was there with bird feathers
and pelicans, and if you needed all this
as much as I once did you'd be devoured
by too much gladness. That's what we were taught
in our windblown Cape Cods
by my own immigrants. In Russia, they said,
we would dance on air for an overcoat
and a thimble full of Slivovitz.

IN VIENNA

Do I not deserve a place on this earth?
　　　　　　　　—Franz Schubert's last words

Schubert and I were strolling through the woods,
hand in hand. He was so syphilitic
you couldn't hear his songs through the coughing.
I didn't want to hurt his feelings:
I wanted to go back to the beer hall, hear him
noodle on the piano, but his sickness was so human
and delinquent it dismantled me: he turned somber
and wistful, like his last sonatas and quartets.
They too were unlistenable unless you had to know
what it felt like, and I don't want to go
to his brother's apartment where he'll end up
penniless, still full of sketches. How can it be
that Vienna surged with melodies without him?
Schubert, my friend from another century.

MUSIC

1.

Whatever else happens
when we listen to music, whether it's Coltrane's
A Love Supreme or Kendrick Lamar's
To Pimp a Butterfly, whether it hints at birdsong
or the dentist's drill, these melodies
take us through flurries of delights, or, in a minor key,
longings and laments. For a moment we feel
what they must feel. At least some of the brain waves
once followed me home from a concert in Cincinnati.

2.

When we tap a rhythm, music activates the cortex
and the cerebellum. The brain strings together
movement, attention, and memory:
it sparks expectation, euphoria, and craving.

3.

I know we can be distracted by
the most trivial of details, we spend too much time
brooding in our own dark caverns,

but isn't the brain marvelous, the way it sits
inside and outside of us as it sets us to dancing
in a hall of strangers? It's so much work
being a person, wrestling with our shadows,
rattling on and on about what distresses us,
I'm all for music pulling the strings,
and if I look like a puppet, jerking my arms about,
I'm just working hard, learning how to listen.

DEATHBED CONFESSION

I don't regret the sailboat I never got when I was ten.
That I might have made a great psychiatrist.
Or holed up in Tuscany instead of Schenectady.
Mastered the clarinet. My only lament is I was less

than joyful. I could have used more bliss.
You know how many years I walked in circles
holding up signs? This war, that war, this Dow,
that Walmart? Pfizer, you're next! There are sharks

that sing to me of their extinction.
Those gardenias by Billie Holiday's headstone,
they're mine. I've taken to singing the last aria
of Traviata with Violetta magically cured.

Now you might not like the music I like, the music
I make: it might sound like pots and pans
banged together, a technique perfected by grandma Eva
of Bialystok to bring us home from danger.

She understood, with her chorus
of *oy veys*, just how wrong everything could be.
She was a friend to the helpless, feckless,
the miserable bastard I could be, readying me

for every allergy, every bee sting, my bright future
in a self-made monastery. But I won't
be pulled along by some donkey with a plow,
I don't want to cash in my bonds

to buy a pontoon and putt-putt through lagoons
on Sunday afternoons. I want a good Côtes du Rhône,
nothing fancy, a little Bird, a smelly cheese,
a few strokes from my beloved if there's one in the room.

And laugh tracks from Buster Keaton's silent films.

EMENDATION

I don't have to go back
to my childhood, there's nothing there
I still want: but of miracles
left to me, I'd like to restore a look
I once wore and release it in the air.

That year I found painting and hiking,
I read all night long, struggling
with *my place in the universe*. Climbing
rock by rock to the Knife Edge
and taking in the aged panorama.

I fell in love almost daily: everyone
was enthralling if you truly looked at them.
Each had a mother, a few had lost
their fathers early. They too heard shouts
in their houses. How dear they are,

even if amour's hammered out of them.
Those faces: rugged and turgid
as they've become, if they've endured,
a boy or girl inside still calls,
Come back, come back and save us.

THE FUTURE

In a flash I cross the centuries.
On my moonwalk no distress

stirs the airless air. No gadgets
please: I'm thinking. A thing

is inarguably a thing: it floats
before my attention span

common as a passing car
with a person in it, gone now

but surfacing in a sweater,
a letter, a nightmare

that sings to me all day. Here
there's no atmosphere,

no suggestion of lack
nor excess. No sun shining,

no light promising,
nothing to look forward to.

no light promising, nothing
to look forward to. Is this

the crystalline state, delicate
as an infant's fingers, friends ask for?

SELF-PORTRAIT WITH BILL EVANS AT THE VANGUARD

It takes a few notes, a very few notes, to undo the bare bones of a person. Where formerly we were piecework in a garment factory, we're now a cache of minor keys: some cerulean, some midnight blue, a few redacted, *Re: The Person We Knew*: 1961 at the Village Vanguard. Hegel holds that the soul is the *form*, the *essence* of any living thing; it is not a substance separate from the body that holds it; the possession of soul turns an organism into an organism; a body without a soul is merely a soul in the wrong body. Our repetitions, our disguises, those cloudy sequences where we're adrift, will bring us to a neighborhood where tulips are sold, where this season's dresses rattle down the street on steel racks. To a basement café where his spare melody stitches us together.

IN THE AVIARY

I could never sit in one place
until I spent a whole afternoon with canaries,
then one with the parrots, then two days with the cockatoos.
In the aviary birds are always flying—into nets,
plexiglass—swooping down to a branch, pecking free
an insect from the bark. They are not always
singing, but when they do, it's rarely in a minor key.
And their stillness we take as a sign of trust.
With all their colors, their preening
of themselves and each other, they must think
they matter. Before them I was always moving
on to the next thing. *And Yet*
had been my mantra. But I am neither subject
nor object of their meanders. I spend my days
invisible in this cinema of the tropics
under the great tent of a sealed-up universe.

I APOLOGIZE IN ADVANCE

but nothing delights me more than eating pussy.
More than imaginary strolls with Picasso
or the yellow sea that swirls in that hot panang curry.

If you've lived in the world, you know there's little wisdom
to dispense: you learn to duck arrows from whichever empire
scribbles down your thoughts before you dream them.

In the end maybe you get one idea to keep to yourself,
but who's to say it's yours? Our minds are little magnets,
bad radios with competing voices from Cincinnati

and Chicago. As for eating pussy, it takes complete trust
in the tongue, complete concentration, opening up
for someone you love: those unfathomable moans give way

to whines and whispers before slipping into sighs
and melody. I mean the whole body becomes a dancer's
body: sinewy, lithe, satin. And once you've stripped down

the niceties and icicles that make us models of decorum,
you can open the window and your neighbors' voices
seem startlingly human. Trivial and impossible.

STORY

In the story where I'm gone,
invisible, forgotten, finally one of many,
I'm hovering over my small town,
the gym, the grocery where the cashier
works three jobs, where the wine merchant
and realtor—who've struggled with their weight
and hearts, as so many of us have struggled—
now perform their song and dance.
And since this is a story I'm flying
over apple orchards and airports, soldiers
at their posts, rows of redbuds, gliding
over cities, voices calling out to one another—
can't you hear them?—some twisting in their sleep,
but even more turning down the sheets,
and now there are clouds, at last there's nothing
human beyond the dirt, the roots, where
of course I'll be, neither gracious nor bitter,
among my neighbors. Once and for all
we're less alone with each other, but where's
the singing, where are street signs, where are you?

A MOMENT'S CALM

I live in my house as I live inside my skin: I know more beautiful,
more ample, more sturdy and more picturesque skins: but it would
seem to me unnatural to exchange them for mine.
—Primo Levi

Now for a moment's calm. Maybe it will go on
and on, like a Strindberg play,
or it could be brief, shockingly brief, like a life.

Maybe I've been waiting my whole life for this.
What I call waiting is settling into a barn
with a ceiling fan to circulate the heated air,

wood beams from another century. In this stillness
I'm not disposed to making corrections.
I'm at peace with your happiness even if you're gone,

even if we fought over which empire owns us,
whose soul is greater, Stravinsky
or Satchmo, or all things that matter less than that.

THE WORD BEAUTIFUL

is exhausted, drained of meaning; it's a bromide,
a cipher, it fills a space better left
in its pen growling, although there's nothing
more beautiful than the ruffles of Ingres's mistress's dress,
cloud-like, cerulean, almost painted yesterday.
The details in the tapestry are explorers' maps, her quizzical look
more compelling than any expression we've been given.
Of course there's Liza's cheek, blood-infused,
a shade of peach, her voice half-conscious, on the edge
of calling out, half-distant at the edge of a river,
cupping her hands to drink in the Kennebec
in August when a heron swoops down for trout
above the Wyman Dam. And then
a table set for two, risotto and scent of thyme,
Jane's cabernet, mint and chocolate,
with a finish, as my mother might say,
You could die for. That stillness: a stone fence
before the old house. She opens the door, as in the opening
of all childhood stories. She doesn't ruin it
by being human and pedestrian, by saying something:
just stand there, with your arms open, just like that.

ITHACA

I've been blessed
with a few gusts of wind,
a few loves
to wave good-bye to.
I still think of mother's kitchen,
sorry for tantrums
of way back when. No frost
lodged in me then. In those days
snow spread through town
like an epidemic: how archival
the blankness seemed.
If you flew above
the shell of the old house
it was nothing really:
there was no story
to our little ranch house
so you couldn't hear a thing.

Recent Titles from Alice James Books

Alice James Books is committed to publishing books that matter. The press was founded in 1973 in Boston, Massachusetts as a cooperative, wherein authors performed the day-to-day undertakings of the press. This element remains present today, as authors who publish with the press are invited to collaborate closely in the publication process of their work. AJB remains committed to its founders' original feminist mission, while expanding upon the scope to include all voices and poets who might otherwise go unheard. In keeping with its efforts to build equity and increase inclusivity in publishing and the literary arts, AJB seeks out poets whose writing possesses the range, depth, and ability to cultivate empathy in our world and to dynamically push against silence. The press was named for Alice James, sister to William and Henry, whose extraordinary gift for writing went unrecognized during her lifetime.

Designed by

PAMELA A. CONSOLAZIO

Spark design

PRINTED BY MCNAUGHTON & GUNN